DRAW KAWAII
MYTHICAL CREATURES

Hatch

First published in the UK in 2021
by The Salariya Book Company Ltd
This edition published in the UK in 2025 by Hatch Press,
an imprint of Bonnier Books UK
4th Floor, Victoria House
Bloomsbury Square, London WC1B 4DA
Owned by Bonnier Books
Sveavägen 56, Stockholm, Sweden
www.bonnierbooks.co.uk

Copyright © 2025 by Hatch Press

1 3 5 7 9 10 8 6 4 2

All rights reserved

ISBN 978-1-83587-271-0

Edited by Rebecca Kealy
Production by Nick Read

Printed in India

DRAW KAWAII
MYTHICAL CREATURES
Step-by-Step

By Isobel Lundie

Hatch

Contents

5. Introduction
6. Materials
8. Making everything cute
10. Adding features
12. Expressions
13. Mixed-up creatures
14. Now it's your turn
16. Kawaii goblin
18. Kawaii elf
20. Kawaii sea monster
22. Kawaii sphinx
24. Kawaii fairy
26. Kawaii yeti
28. Kawaii vampire
30. Kawaii dragon
32. Kawaii minotaur
34. Kawaii unicorn
36. Kawaii gnome
38. Kawaii cyclops
40. Kawaii mermaid
42. Kawaii ghost
44. Kawaii monster
46. Kawaii pixie
48. Kawaii werewolf
50. Kawaii devil
52. Kawaii zombie
54. Kawaii griffin
56. Kawaii mummy
58. Kawaii troll
60. Kawaii centaur
62. Kawaii Loch Ness monster
64. Glossary

Introduction
what is kawaii?

Kawaii means 'cute' in the Japanese language but a Japanese art style has evolved which is also known as 'kawaii'. This style emphasises the 'cuteness' of the characters it depicts.

This book shows you how to master the techniques required to draw your own 'kawaii' creatures. It includes tips and general information before you start and then a series of step-by-step projects for you to follow.

Materials

Pencil
Drawing with an HB pencil makes it easy to erase any unwanted excess lines.

Materials
The ideas in this book can be done in different ways and with different materials. Here are some suggestions.

Coloured paper
Try drawing kawaii animals on coloured paper!

Coloured pencils
Coloured pencils are ideal for shading and creating texture. Take a look at this drawing of a goblin.

Labels
Make your own kawaii labels to add to presents.

Ink
Use a small brush to make cute inky paintings!

Stickers
Draw onto stickers to make cute drawings for your friends!

Sketchbook
Use a sketchbook so that you can keep all your drawings together.

Making everything cute

Soften shapes
Rounding off the points of a triangle softens its shape. Try softening the edges of shapes when drawing your kawaii characters.

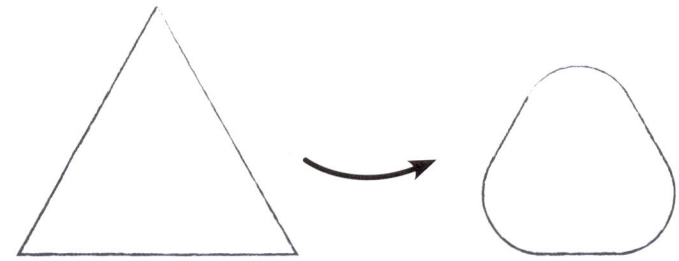

Simplify drawings
Make your drawing cuter by simplifying it down to its key features. This way you can make almost anything cute!

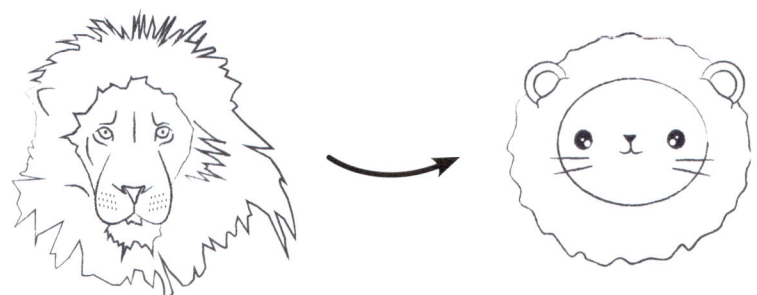

Proportions
The kawaii body should be proportioned as shown. A large head, with a short body and short legs.

Add a cute face

You can make almost anything cute by drawing an adorable cartoon face on it.

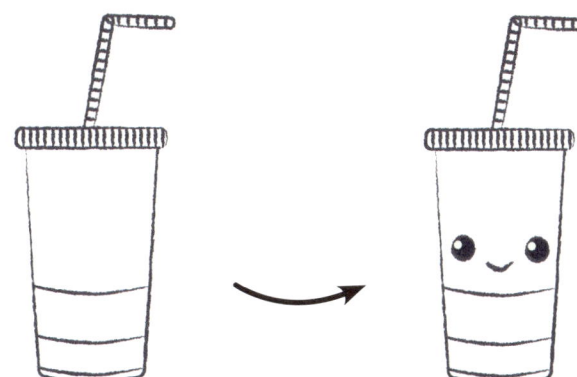

Colours to soften

Pastel colours are softer. Try using less saturated shades to make your characters cuter.

Motion lines

Adding motion lines in this way is a simple and effective way to convey movement in a drawing.

Adding features

Cute feet
Adding adorable feet to your characters is a good way to make them look even cuter.

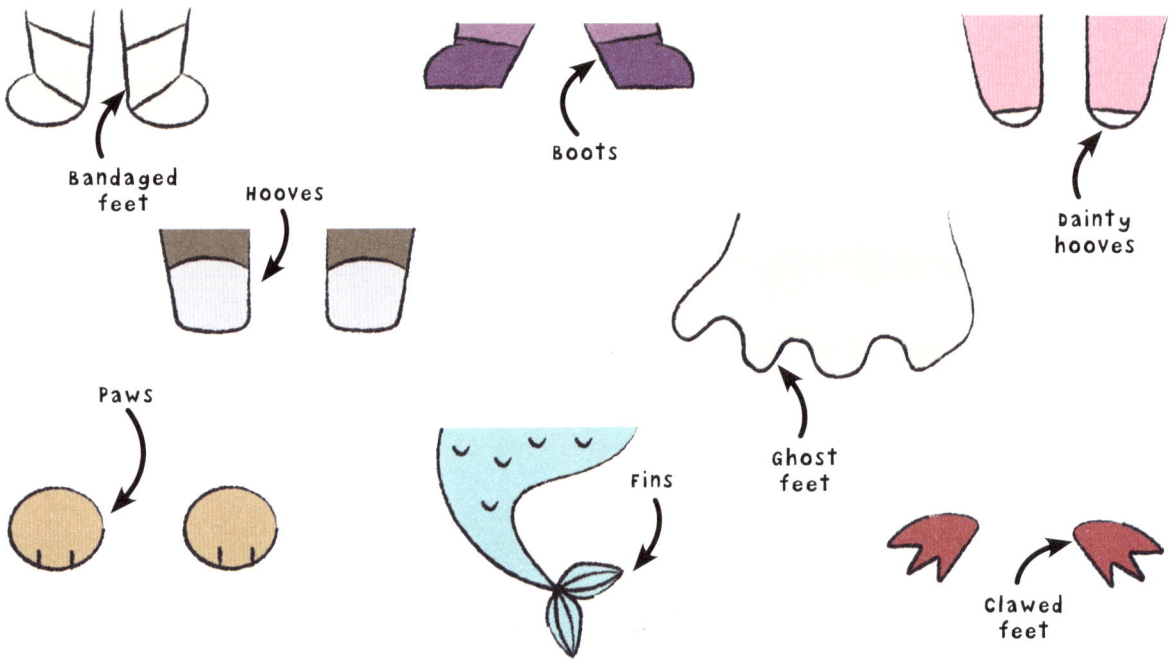

Cute stuff
Don't forget that objects can help to bring a character to life!

Cute features

Animals have all manner of distinguishing features, from fluffy ears to horns! You'll need to get to know them all in order to draw them.

Expressions

Changing your character's expression adds personality.

Happy
Draw happy 'U'-shaped eyes.

Sad
Draw curved eyebrows.

Angry
Draw diagonal eyebrows.

Confused
Draw one eyebrow raised.

Scared
Raise both eyebrows.

Excited
Draw the mouth wider.

Silly
Play with the eyebrows and stick the tongue out.

Tired
Draw the eyes closed.

Embarrassed
Draw a pursed mouth and red cheeks.

Mixed-up creatures

Can you use the features on the previous page to create your own mixed-up creature faces?

Now it's your turn!

Kawaii goblin

Draw your own goblin!

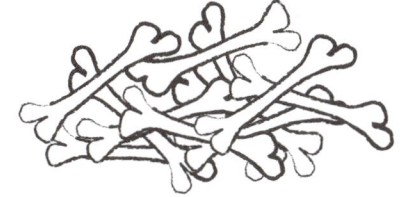

Why not draw your kawaii elf working in Santa's workshop?

Kawaii elf

Draw your own elf.

Kawaii sea monster

Draw your own sea monster.

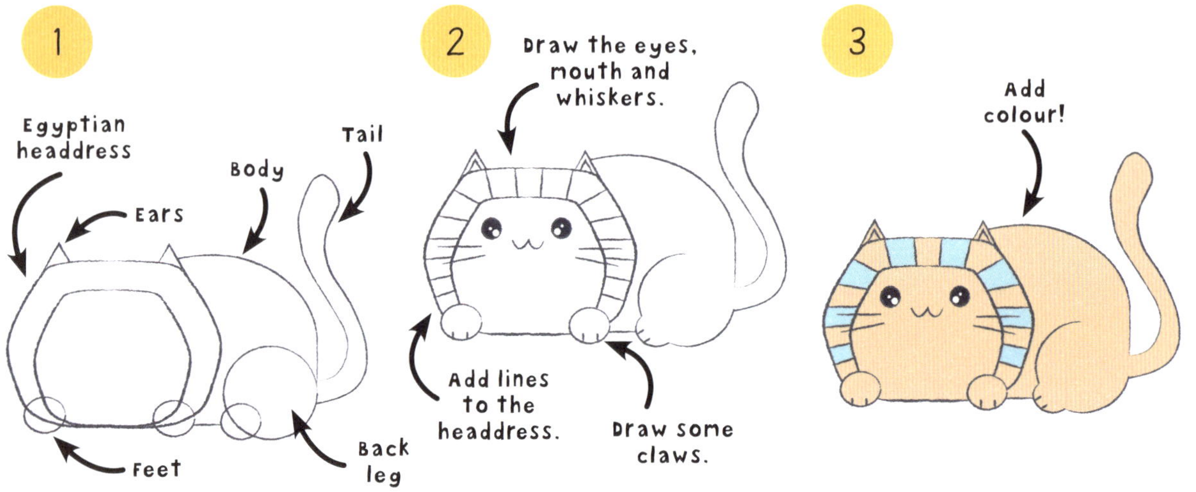

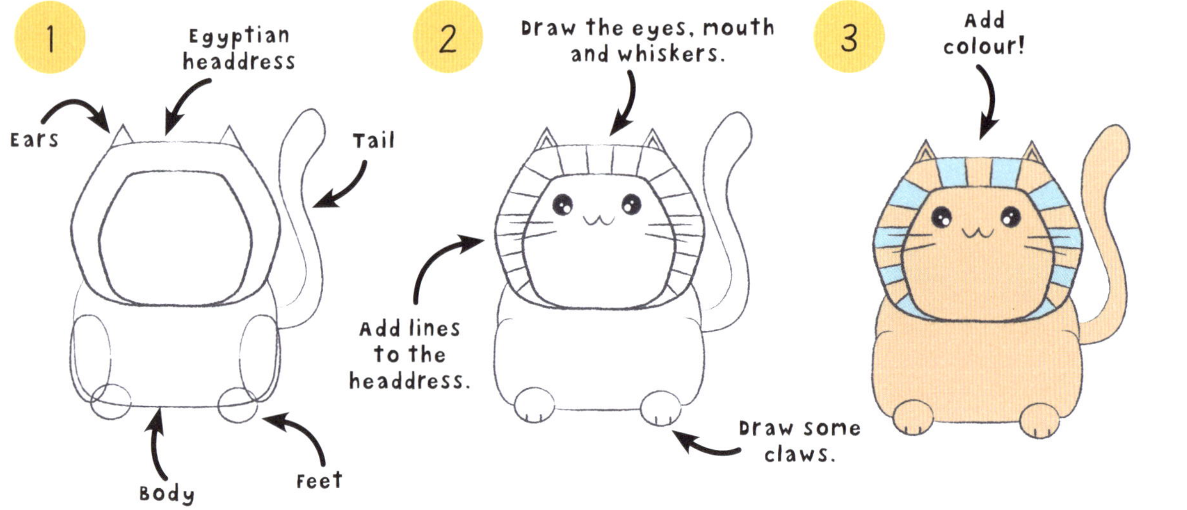

1
- Egyptian headdress
- Ears
- Body
- Tail
- Feet
- Back leg

2
Draw the eyes, mouth and whiskers.
Add lines to the headdress.
Draw some claws.

3
Add colour!

1
- Ears
- Egyptian headdress
- Tail
- Body
- Feet

2
Draw the eyes, mouth and whiskers.
Add lines to the headdress.
Draw some claws.

3
Add colour!

Why not draw your kawaii Sphinx crouching in a desert landscape?

22

Kawaii sphinx

Draw your own sphinx.

Kawaii fairy

Draw your
own fairy.

25

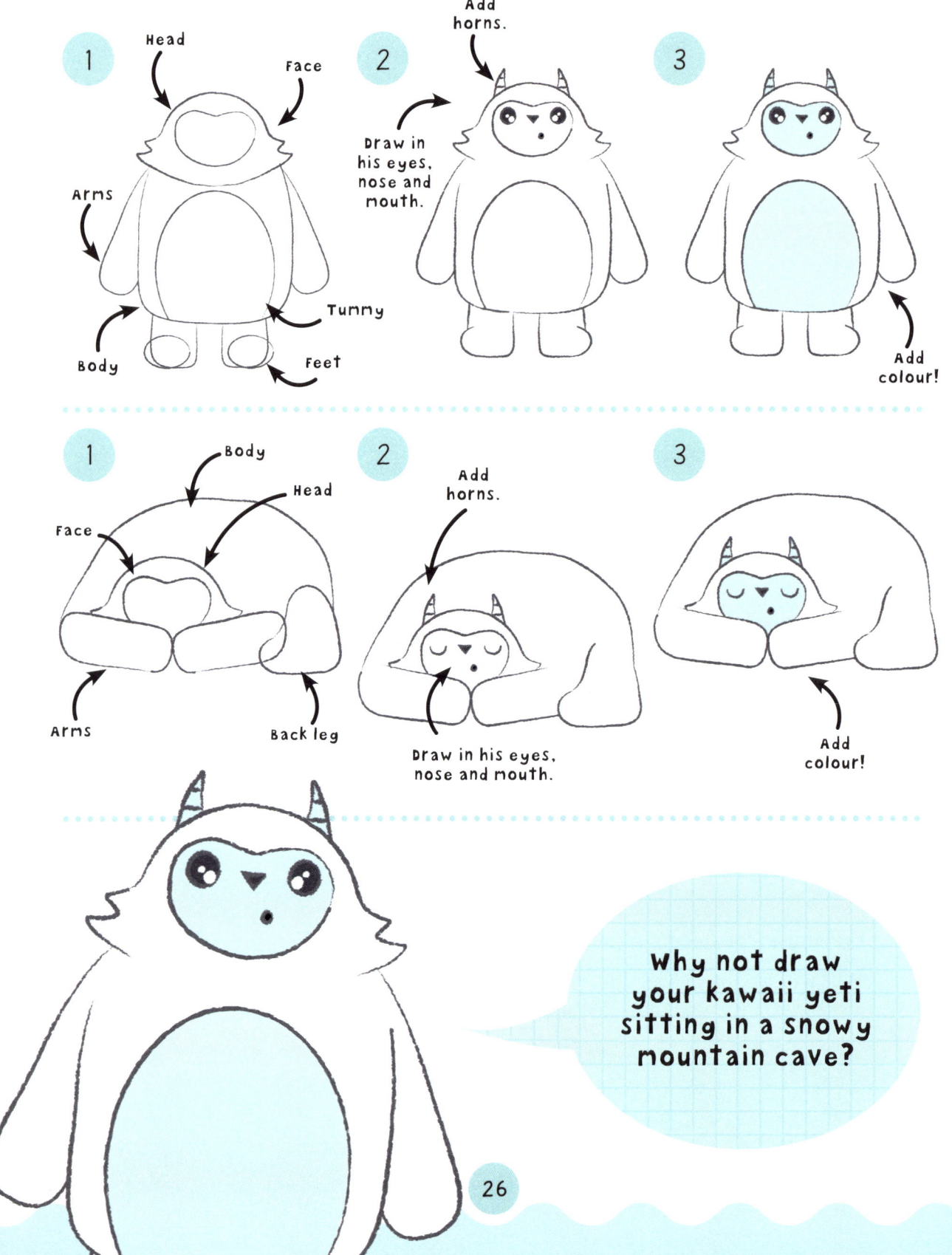

Kawaii yeti

Draw your own yeti.

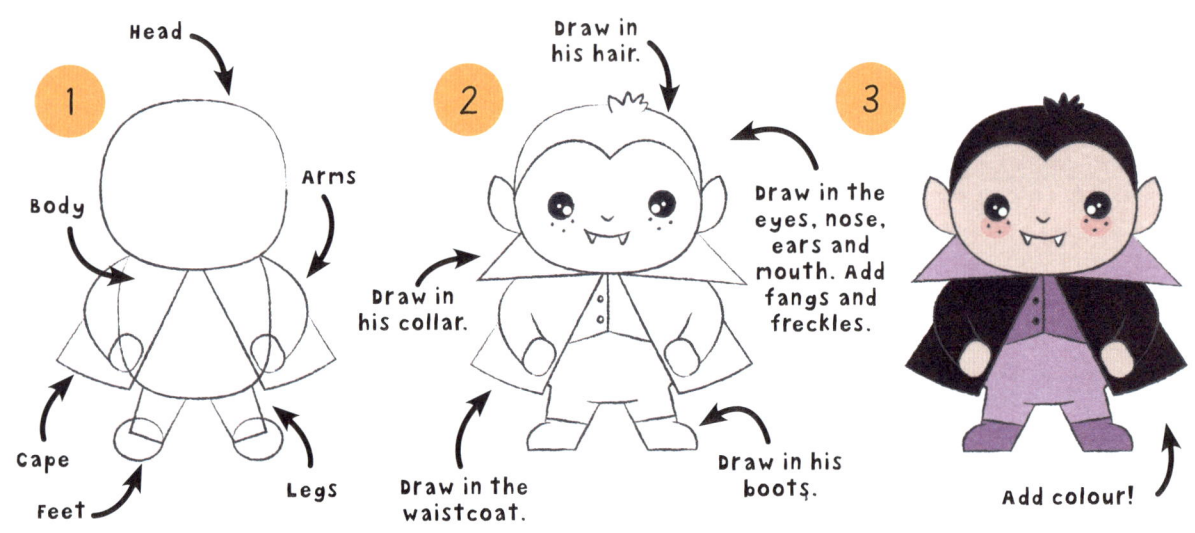

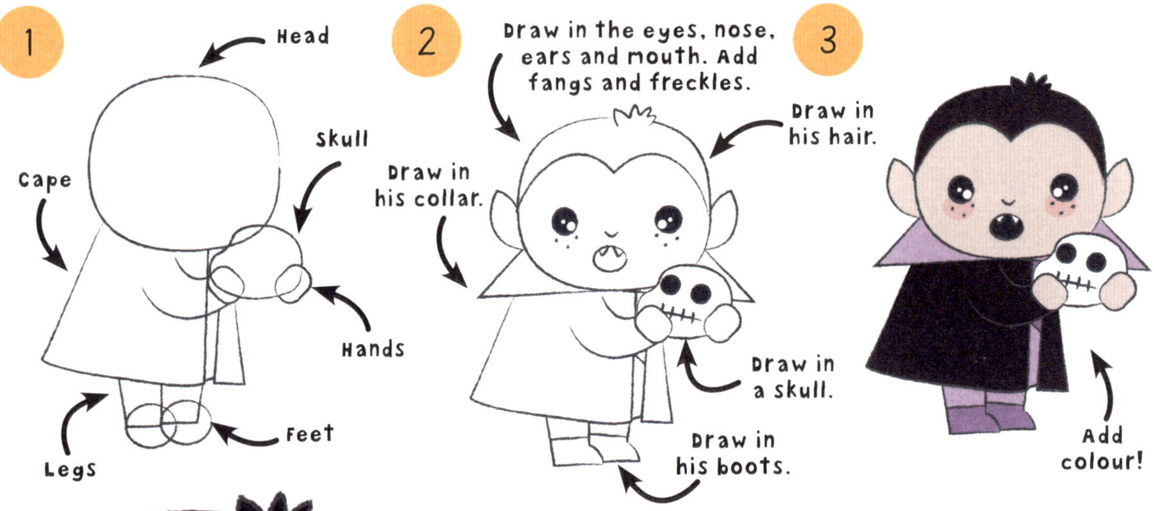

Why not draw your kawaii vampire hanging upside down in his crumbling castle?

Kawaii Vampire

Draw your own vampire.

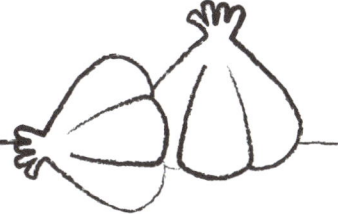

Why not draw your kawaii dragon guarding a giant treasure trove?

Kawaii dragon

Draw your own dragon.

Kawaii minotaur

Draw your own minotaur.

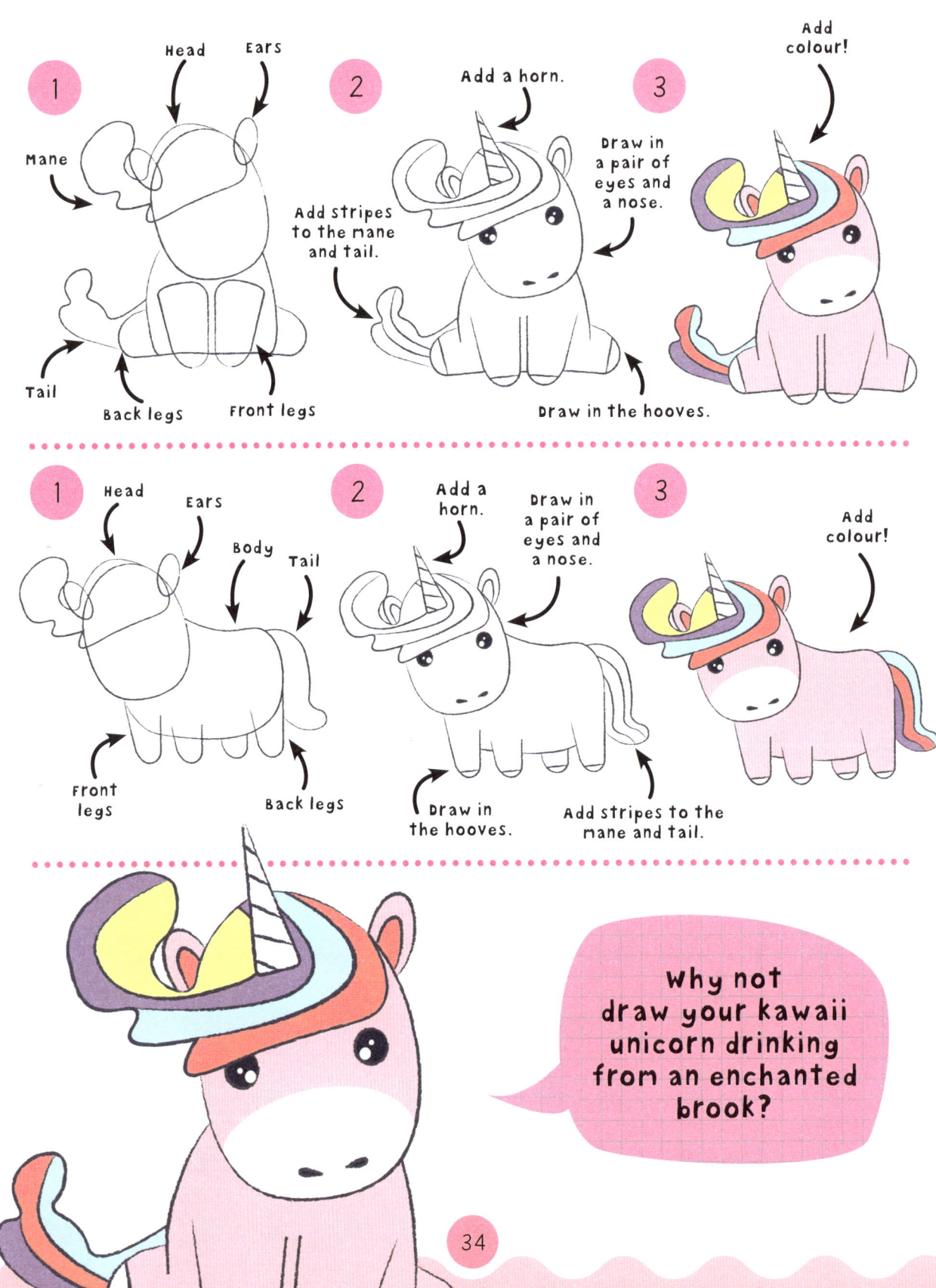

Kawaii unicorn

Draw your own unicorn.

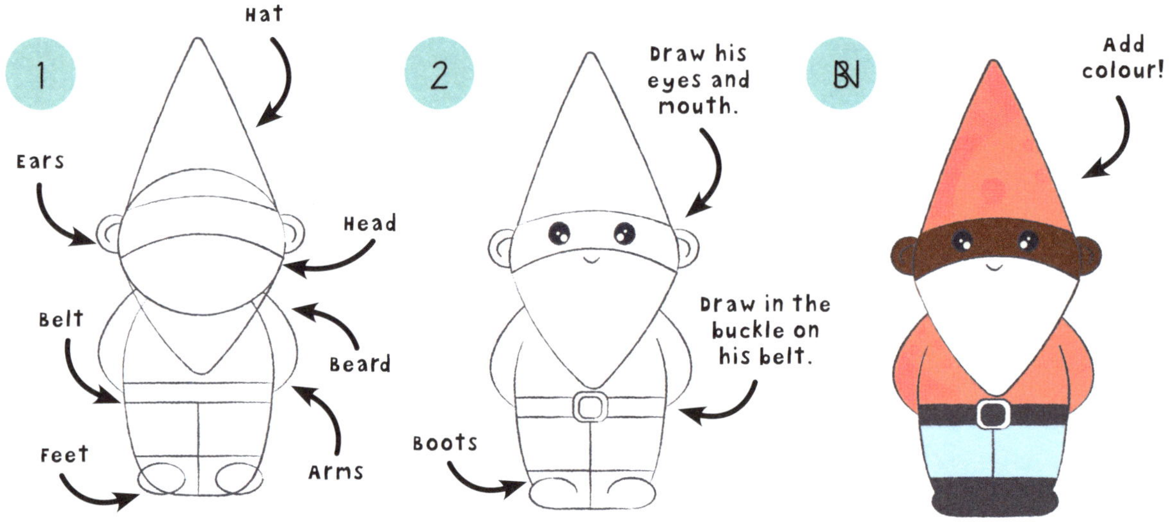

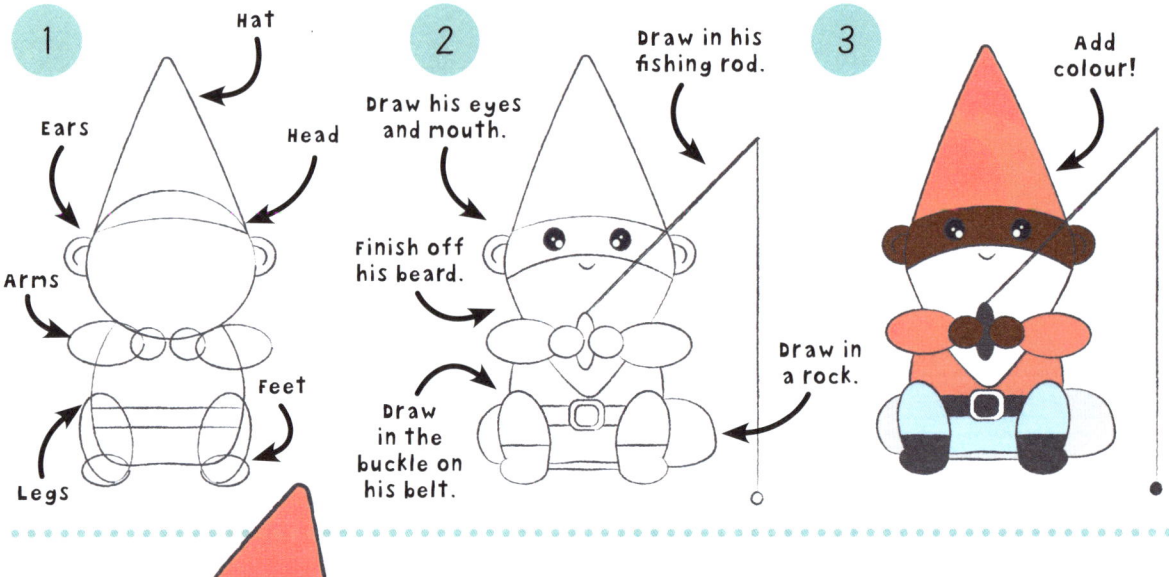

Why not draw your kawaii gnome fishing on a sleepy riverbank?

Kawaii gnome

Draw your own gnome.

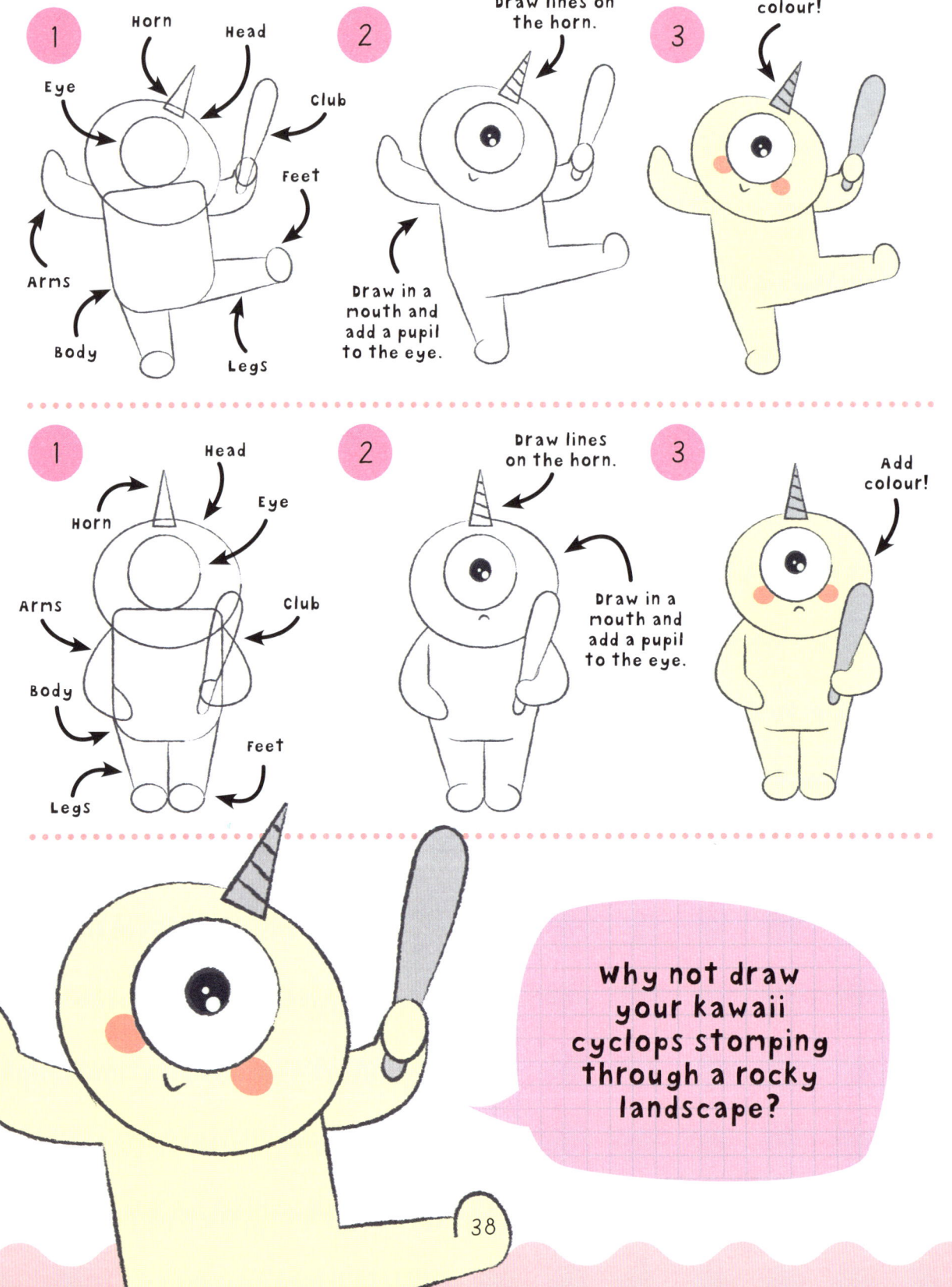

Kawaii cyclops

Draw your own cyclops.

Kawaii mermaid

Draw your own mermaid.

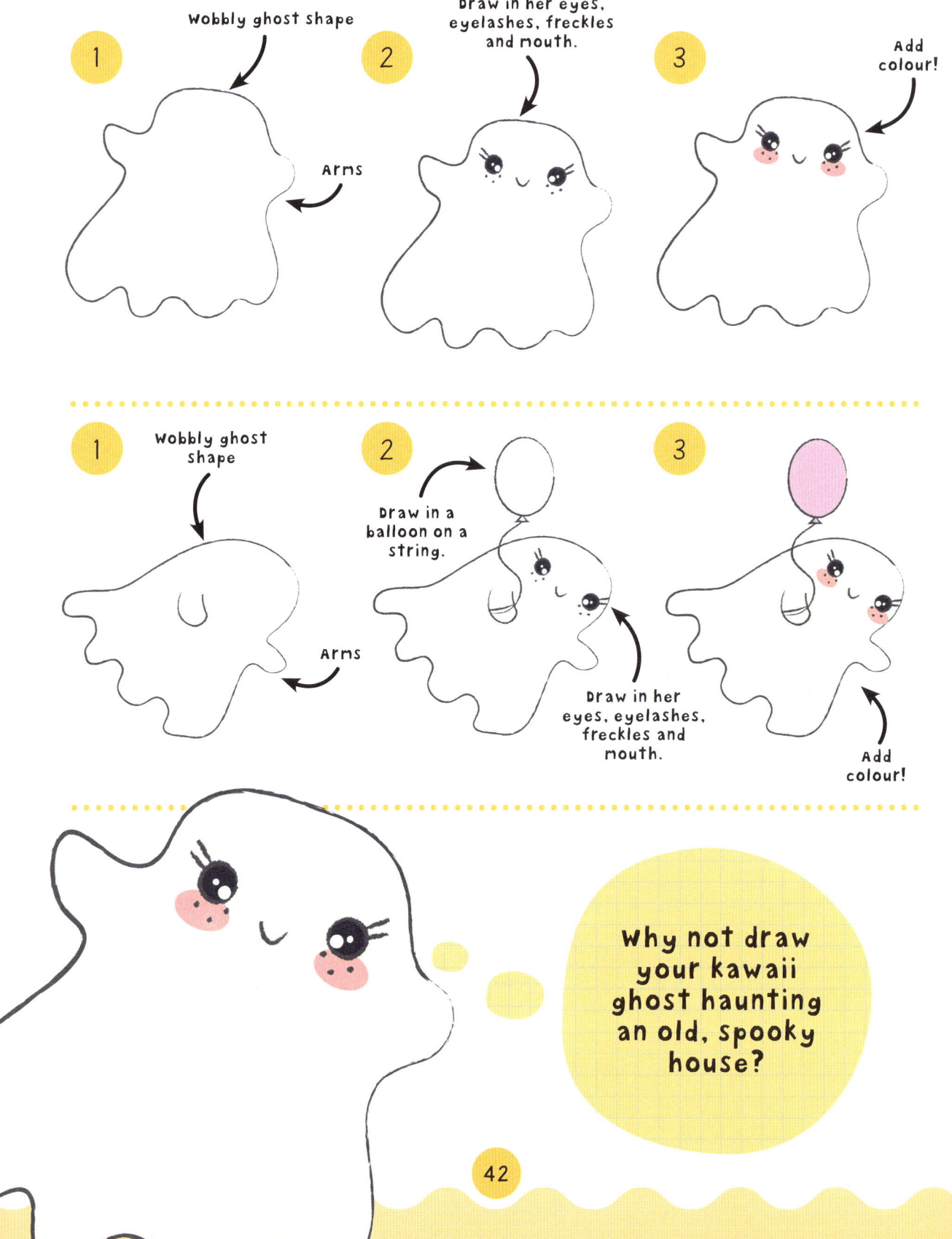

Kawaii ghost

Draw your own ghost.

Kawaii monster

Draw your own monster.

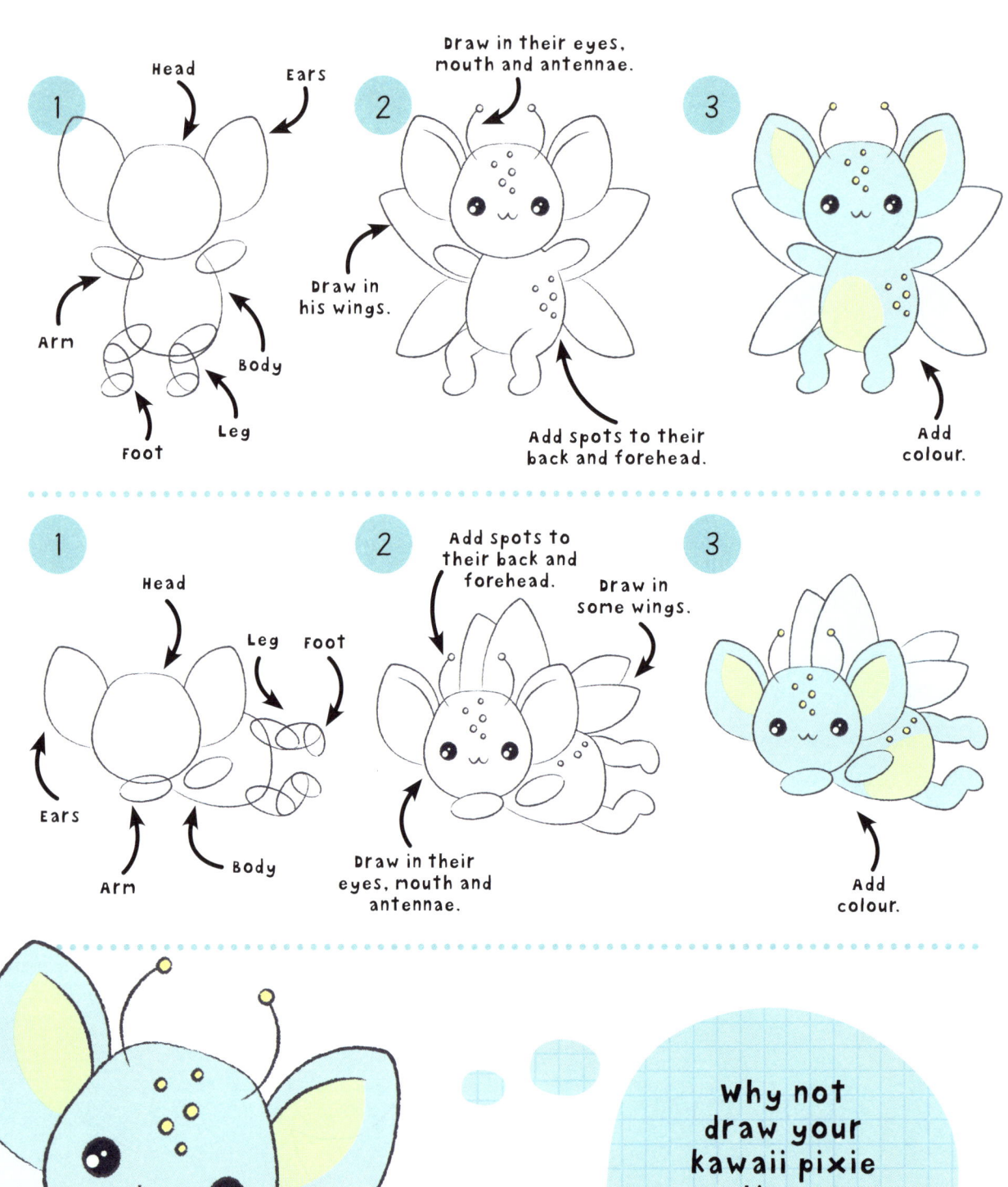

Kawaii pixie

Draw your own pixie.

Kawaii werewolf

Draw your own werewolf.

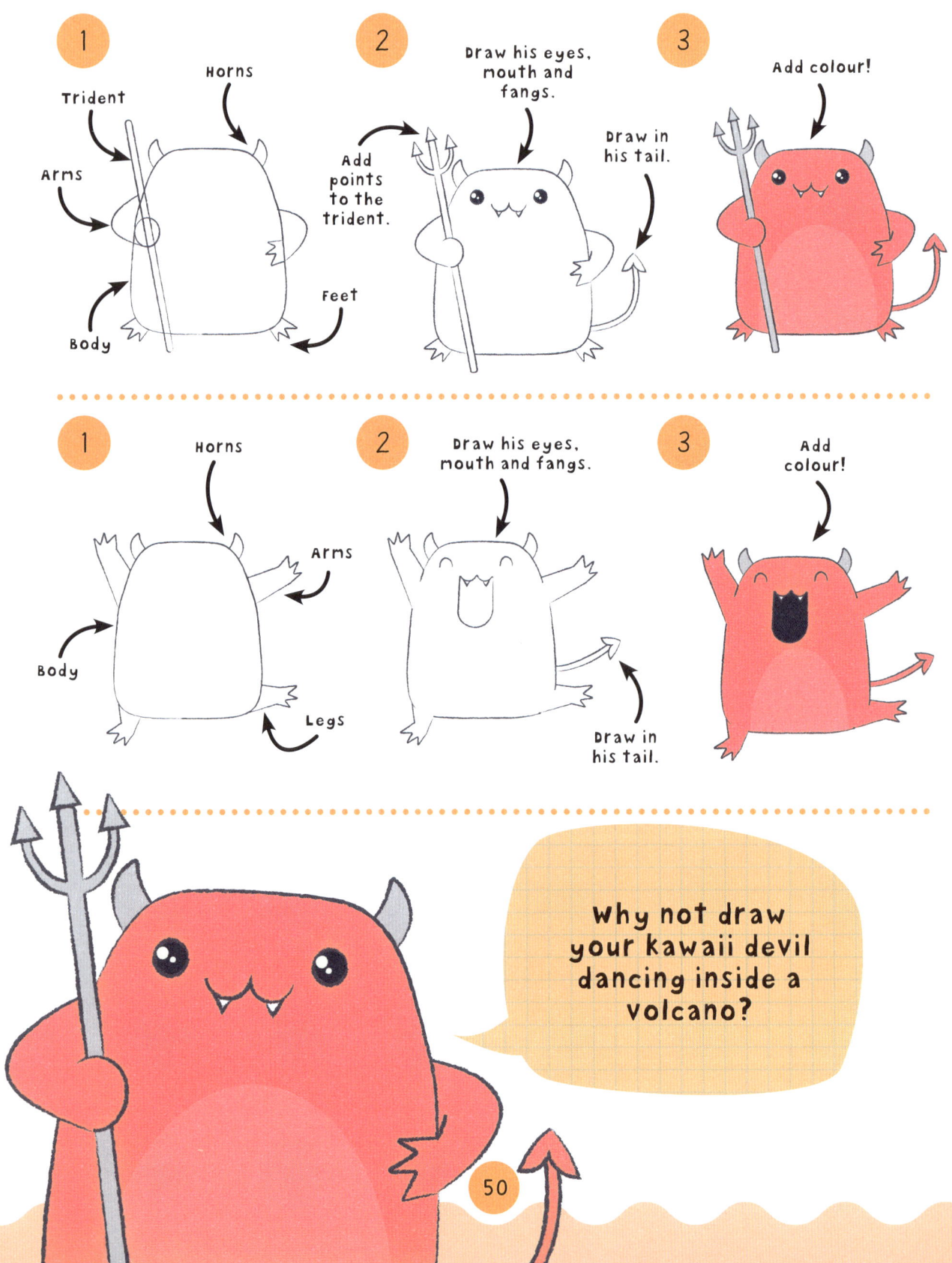

Kawaii devil

Draw your own devil.

Kawaii zombie

Draw your own zombie.

Kawaii griffin

Draw your own griffin.

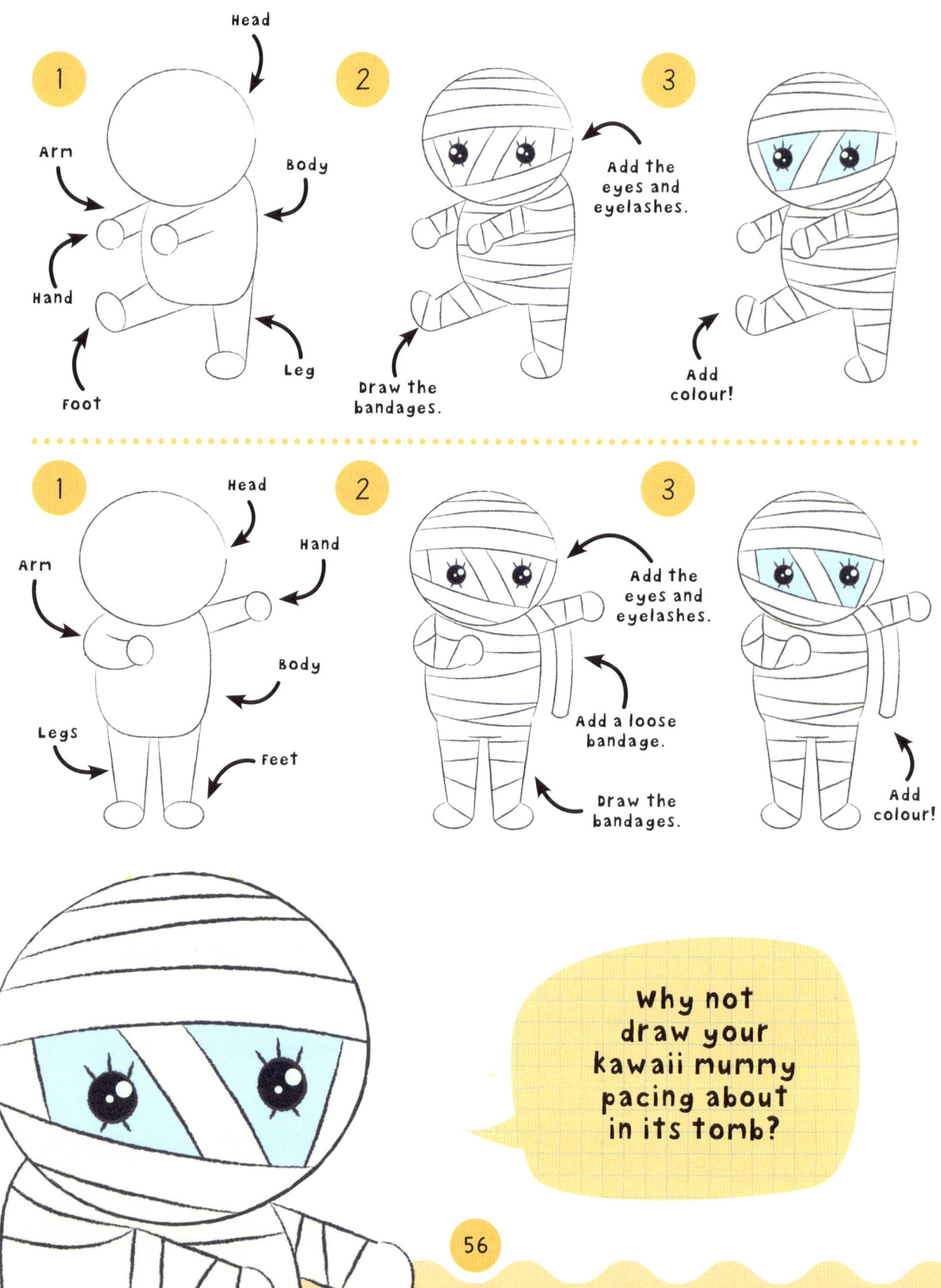

Kawaii mummy

Draw your own mummy.

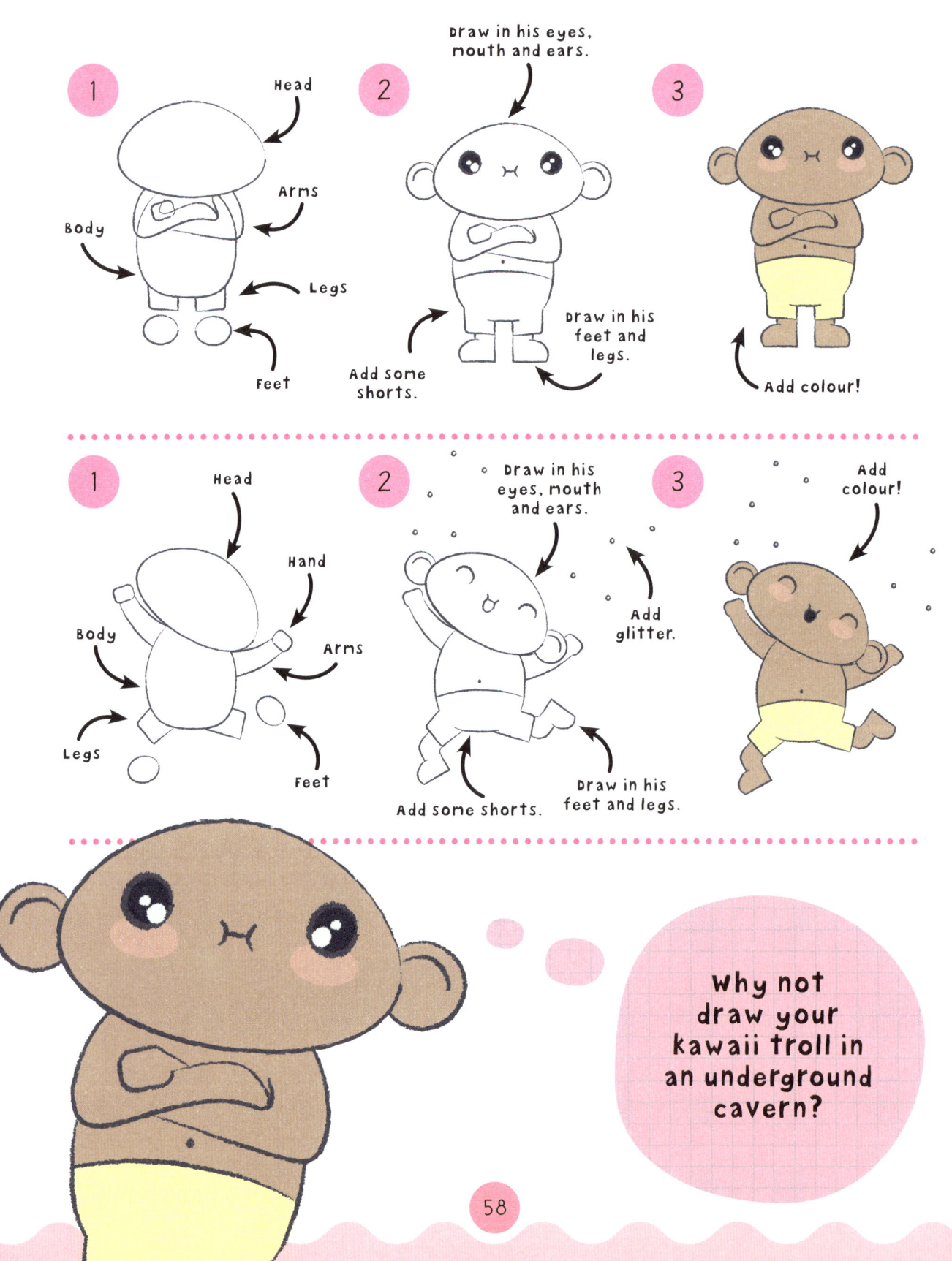

Kawaii troll

Draw your
own troll.

Kawaii centaur

Draw your own centaur.

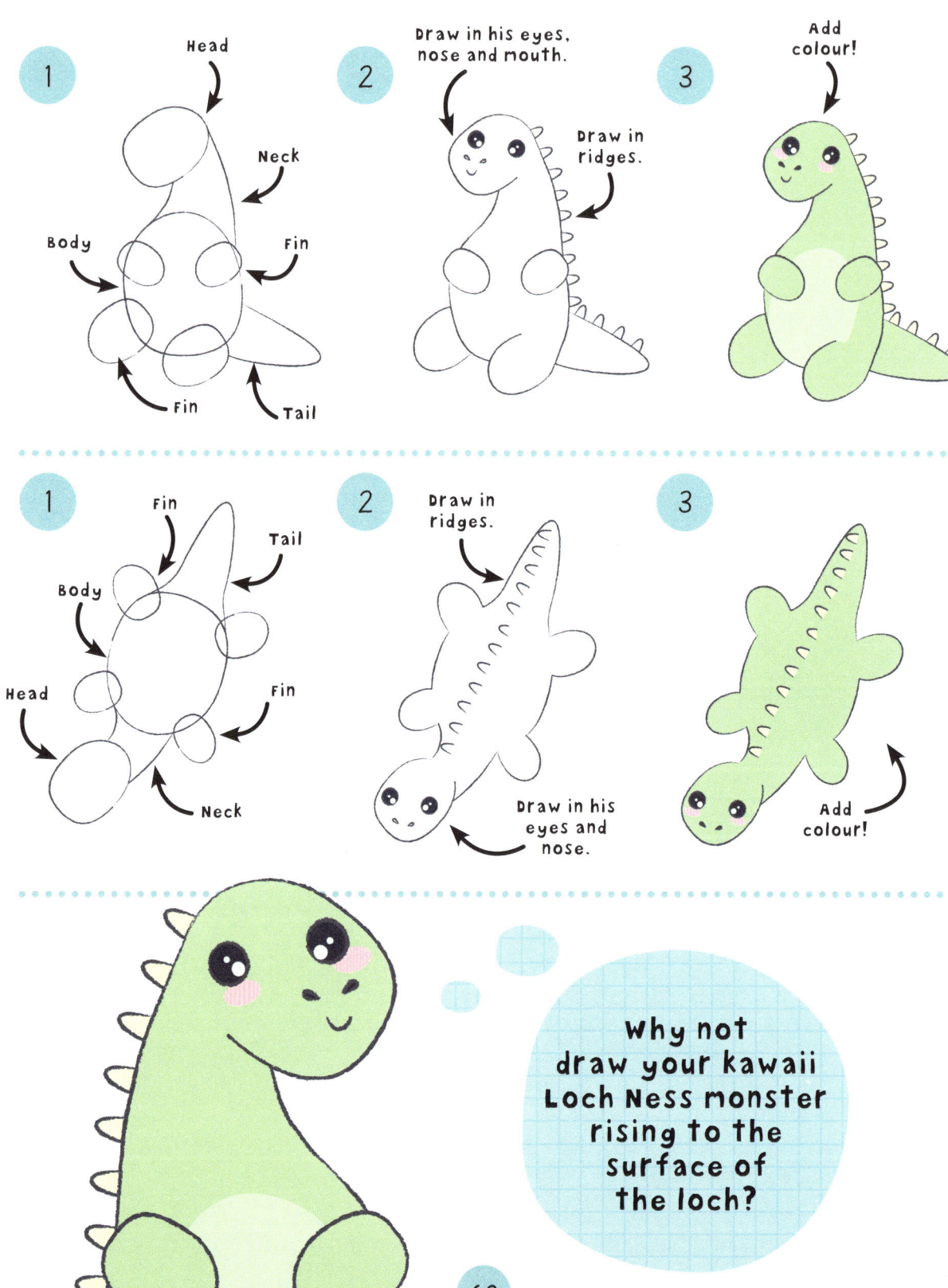

Kawaii Loch Ness monster

Draw your own
Loch Ness monster.

Glossary

Antennae These are special feelers that some insects and other animals have on their heads. Insects use their antennae to smell, feel and sense things in their environment.

Centaur From Greek mythology, with the upper body of a human and the lower body and legs of a horse. Centaurs are known for being skilled archers and living in the forests and hills.

Cyclops A giant from Greek myths with just one big eye in the middle of their forehead.

Griffin A mythical creature with the head of a lion and the wings and body of an eagle.

Labyrinth A maze.

Loch Scots word for a lake.

Pastel Shades of colour that are soft and gentle. Pastel colours are made with pastel crayons.

Quiff A hairstyle where the front of the hair is brushed upwards and back, making a wave or curl.

Sphinx A mythical creature with the body of a lion and the head of a human.

Trident A three-pronged spear.

Yeti A mythical large, hairy creature from snowy mountains, sometimes called the Abominable Snowman.